THE HYMNS PROJECT

JONATHAN VEIRA

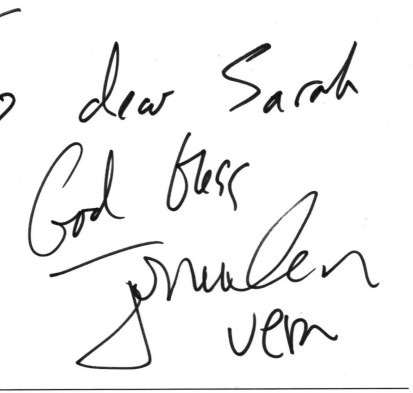

To dear Sarah
God bless
Jonathan
Veira

12 much-loved hymns
with new and familiar melodies

PIANO-VOCAL SCORES

ACKNOWLEDGEMENTS
Music typesetting: David Ball
Artwork: beatroot.media
Project Co-Ordinators: Denise Anstead & Sue Rinaldi
A&R: Sue Rinaldi
Executive Producer: Peter Martin

Thanks to Jonathan Veira for song notes content and help on the music scores.

Published & distributed by Essential Christian, 14 Horsted Square, Uckfield, East Sussex, TN22 1QG, UK.
An activity of Memralife Group, Registered Charity number 1126997, a Company limited by guarantee, registered in England and Wales, number 6667924. Registered Office: 14 Horsted Square, Uckfield, East Sussex, TN22 1QG.

ISBN 978-1-911237-09-9

CONTENTS

And Can It Be

CCLI# 7098749

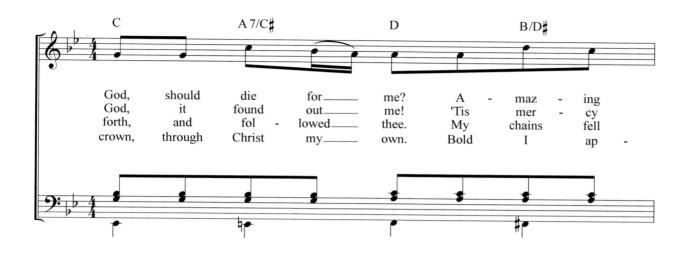

God,   should   die   for____   me?   A - maz - ing
God,   it   found   out____   me!   'Tis   mer - cy
forth,   and   fol - lowed____   thee.   My   chains   fell
crown,   through   Christ   my____   own.   Bold   I   ap -

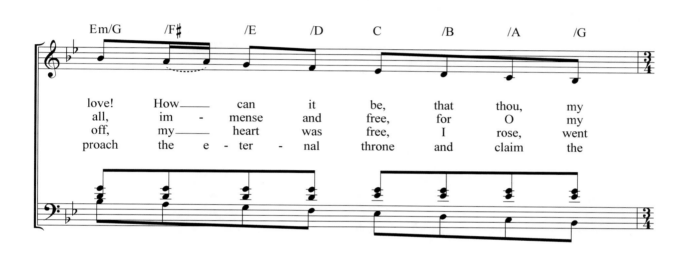

love!   How____   can   it   be,   that   thou,   my
all,   im - mense   and   free,   that   for   O   my
off,   my____   heart   was   free,   I   rose,   went
proach   the   e - ter - nal   throne   and   claim   the

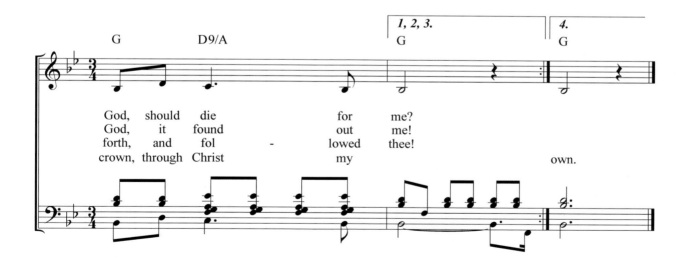

1, 2, 3.   *4.*

God,   should   die   for   me?
God,   it   found   out   me!
forth,   and   fol -   lowed   thee!
crown,   through   Christ   my   own.

Be Still

Key = C

David J Evans

1. Be still, for the pre-sence of the Lord, the Ho - ly One is here;

come bow be - fore him now, with re - ve - rence and fear.

In him no sin is found, we stand on ho - ly ground.

Be still, for the pre-sence of the Lord, the Ho - ly One is here.

CCLI# 120824

2. Be still, for the glo-ry of the Lord is shin-ing all a-

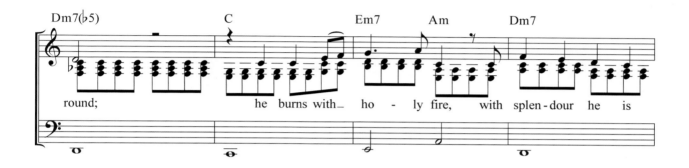

round; he burns with ho-ly fire, with splen-dour he is

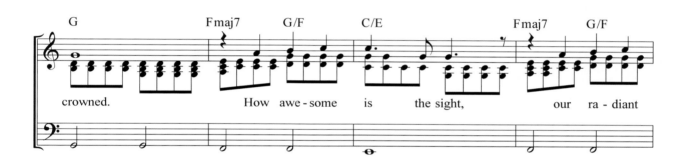

crowned. How awe-some is the sight, our ra-diant

King of light. Be still, for the glo-ry of the Lord is shin-ing all a-

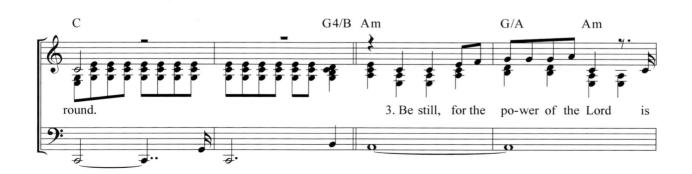

round. 3. Be still, for the po-wer of the Lord is

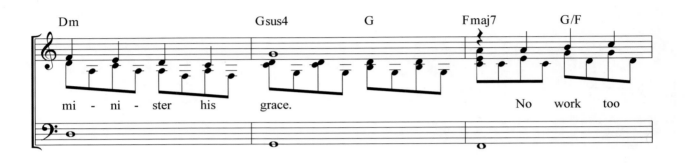

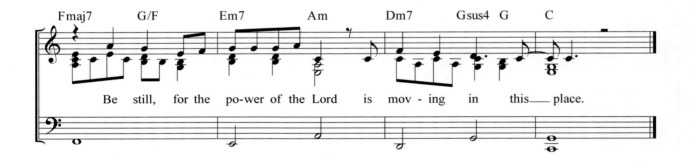

SONG NOTES

by Jonathan Veira

AND CAN IT BE

This hymn was written to celebrate the conversion of Charles Wesley. He had gone through a huge amount to get to this moment of spiritual awakening - including being ordained into the Church Of England with his brother John and going on failed missionary exploits to Georgia before returning home to be persuaded that he required a conversion of his soul. May 21st, 1738 marked his turning point. Charles gathered all his poetic might and Bible knowledge and wrote 'My chains fell off, my heart was free, I rose went forth and followed thee.'

This new tune follows the pacing of the most popular of the tunes we now sing – ebbing and flowing with the lyrics. Sing with great energy and use every crescendo of musical phrase and text.

BE STILL

This perennial favourite, composed in 1989 by David J Evans, is loved by so many in the modern church. Our arrangement gives the song even more space for you to 'Be Still'. The pace is always slower than you think and you will find that the effect is to calm the mind and allow yourself space to hear the still small voice.

I CANNOT TELL

Londonderry Air, popularly known as Danny Boy, is one of the most well-known melodies of all time. It comes from the tradition of Irish folk melodies and is still being sung throughout the world. William Young Fullerton wrote the words as a hymn for young people c1930 – his idea was to take a current popular tune that people would have in their bones and use it to tell the Christian story. Sing with energy and use guitars and melodic instruments - eg flute - to augment the sweetness of the melody. Encourage your congregation to sing with enthusiasm, letting the words 'but this I know' ring in your ears!

I STAND AMAZED

Charles H Gabriel wrote this gospel song in 1898 at a moment in American Protestantism where a new style of popular music was finding its way into the church. The tune is catchy and simple and the theme straightforward and worshipful. Charles was a prolific writer with over 6000 songs to his credit – penning such wonderful songs as *His Eye is on the Sparrow* and *Crown Him with Many Crowns*. Here we have given this a real modern 'Gospel' feel and to that end a band would be useful – particularly bass and drums to add to the standard guitar and keyboard.

I Cannot Tell

Key = B♭

Capo 3 (G)

Unknown/
William Young Fullerton

♩ = c. 66 Freely

1. I can-not tell___ why he, whom an - gels wor - ship, should set his
tell___ how si - lent - ly he suf - fered, as with his
tell___ how all the lands shall wor - ship, when, at his

love___ up on the sons of ___ men, or why, as Shep - herd,
peace___ he graced the place of ___ tears, or how his heart___ up -
bid - ding, ev - 'ry storm is ___ stilled, or who can say___ how

he should seek___ the wan - d'rers, to bring them___ back, they
on the cross___ was bro - ken, the crown of___ pain to
great the ju - bi - la - tion, when all the___ hearts of

know not how___ or when. But this I know,___ he
three and thir - ty years. But this I know,___ all
men with love___ are filled But this I know,___ the

Copyright © Public Domain

CCLI# 4957917

10

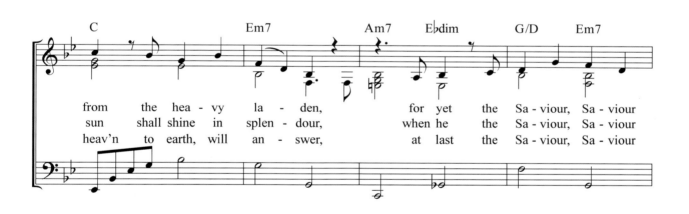

11

I Stand Amazed

Key = F

Charles H Gabriel

CCLI# 25297

Chorus

How mar-vel-lous! How won-der-ful,— and—my song shall e - ver be;—

how mar-vel-lous! How won-der-ful— is my— Sa-viour's— love for—

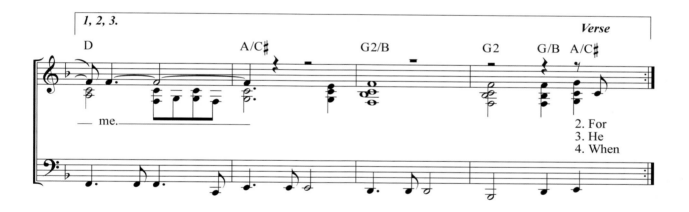

1, 2, 3.

Verse

— me.

2. For
3. He
4. When

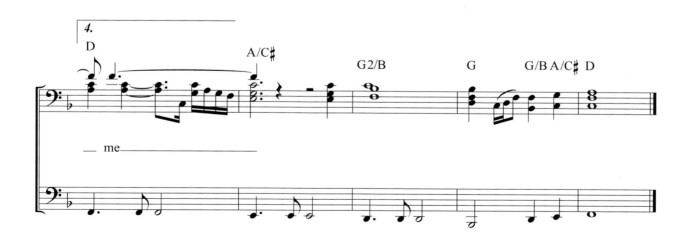

4.

— me—

I Surrender All

Key = D

Judson Wheeler Van DeVenter
& Winfield Scott Weeden

CCLI# 23189

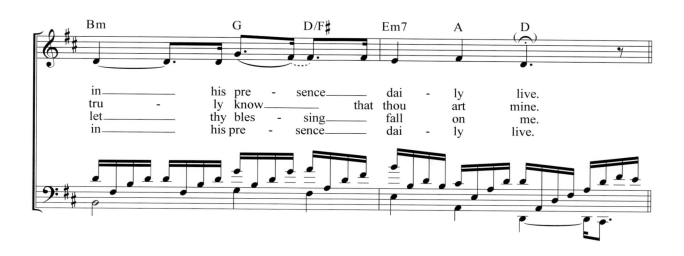

Chorus

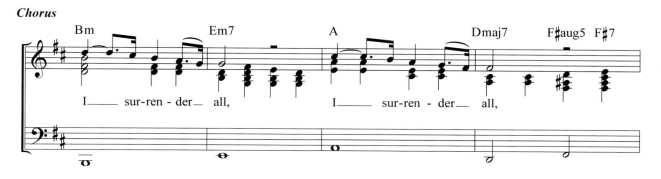

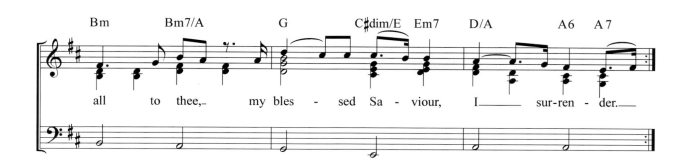

I Will Sing The Wondrous Story

Key = F

Capo 3 (D)

Francis H Rowley
& Rowland Hugh Prichard

♩ = 168

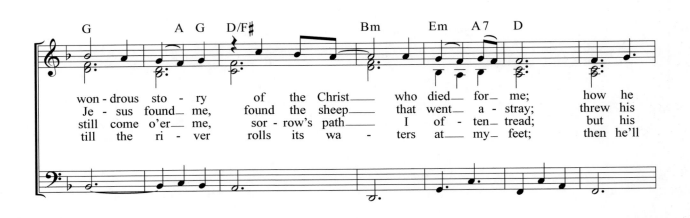

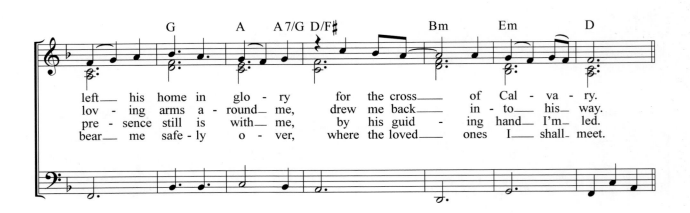

CCLI# 2328610

Chorus

Yes, I'll sing— the won-drous sto - ry of the Christ— who died— for— me;

sing— it with— the saints— in glo - ry ga-thered by— the cry - stal—

1, 2, 3.   *(to v.2,3,4 after repeat)*   *4.*

sea._____   sea.

Joyful, Joyful, We Adore Thee

Key = D

Edward Hodges,
Henry Van Dyke & Ludwig van Beethoven

𝅗𝅥 = 84

1. Joy-ful, joy-ful, we a-dore thee, God of glo-ry,
2. All thy works with joy sur-round thee, earth and heav'n re-

Lord of love; hearts un-fold like flow'rs be-fore thee,
flect thy rays; stars and an-gels sing a-round thee,

op-'ning to the sun a-bove. Melt the clouds of
cen-tre of un-bro-ken praise. Field and fo-rest,

CCLI# 25321

18

sin and sad - ness, drive the dark of doubt_____ a - way;_____
vale and moun - tain, flow - 'ry mea - dow, flash - ing sea,_____

gi - ver of im - mor - tal glad - ness, fill us with the_____
sing-ing bird and flow - ing foun - tain call us to re -

light, of day.
joice in thee.

(Fine)

Just As I Am

Key = E

Original Lyrics: Charlotte Elliott
New Lyrics & Music: Jonathan Veira/Matthew Veira
Arr: Jonathan Veira & Mark Edwards

1. Just as I am, with-out one plea, but that___ your blood was shed___ for me, and that you bid me come to thee. Just as I am, and waiting not to rid my soul of one dark blot. To you whose blood can

as I am, though tossed a-bout, with ma-ny a con-flict, ma-ny a doubt, fight-ings with-in and fears with-out. Just as I am, poor, wret-ched, blind, sight, rich-es, heal-ing of the mind, yes, all I need in

as I am, you will re-ceive; will wel-come, par-don, cleanse,__ re-lieve, be-cause your pro-mise I be-lieve. Just as I am, your love un-known, has bro-ken ev-'ry bar-rier down, now, to be yours, yes

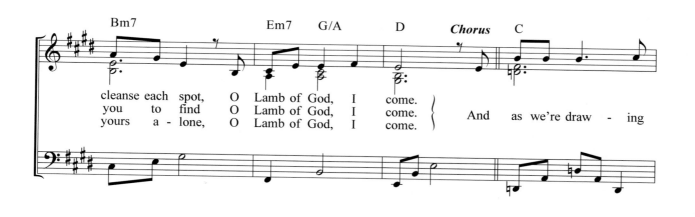

cleanse each spot, O Lamb of God, I come.
you to find O Lamb of God, I come.
yours a - lone, O Lamb of God, I come.

And as we're draw - ing

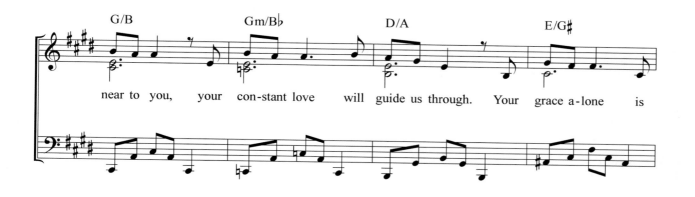

near to you, your con-stant love will guide us through. Your grace a-lone is

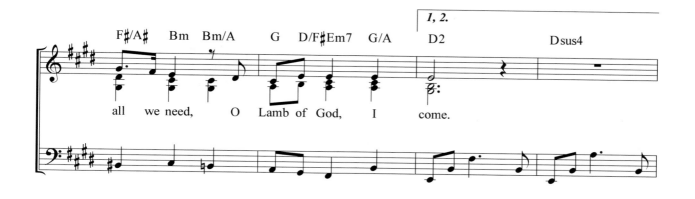

1, 2.

all we need, O Lamb of God, I come.

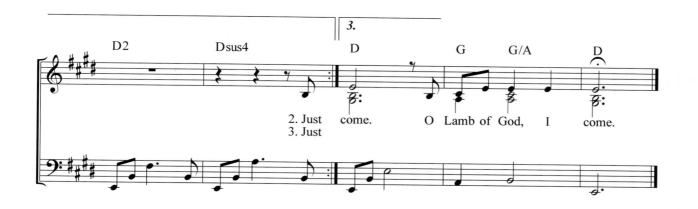

3.

2. Just come. O Lamb of God, I come.
3. Just

Love Divine, All Loves Excelling

Key = E

Words: Charles Wesley
Music: Jonathan Veira
Arr: Jonathan Veira & Mark Edwards

O For A Thousand Tongues

Key = G

Original Lyrics: Charles Wesley
Additional Lyrics & Music: Jonathan Veira/Matthew Veira
Arr: Jonathan Veira & Mark Edwards

all   the earth   a - broad   the ho - nours   of   thy   name.
make   the foul - est clean,   his blood a - vailed for   me.
bro -   ken hearts   re - joice,   the hum - ble poor be - lieve.

And with our

voice   we   sing our songs of praise; with our   hearts   we'll   wor-ship you for all   our

days.

2. Je - sus!   The
3. He speaks, and

days.

25

O Love That Will Not Let Me Go

Key = A

Original Lyrics: George Matheson
New Chorus Lyrics & Music: Jonathan Veira/Susan Veira
Arr: Jonathan Veira & Mark Edwards

1. O love that will not let me go, I
   light that fol-lows all my way, I
   joy that seek-est me through pain, I
   cross that lift-est up my head, I

rest—— my wea-ry soul in thee, I give thee back the life I
yield—— my flick-'ring torch to thee, my heart re-stores its bor-rowed
can-not close my heart to thee, I trace the rain-bow through the
dare—— not ask to fly from thee, I lay in dust life's glo-ry

owe, that in thine o-cean depths its flow may ri-cher,——
ray, that in thy sun-shine's blaze its day, may bright-er,——
rain, and feel the pro-mise is not vain that morn—— shall
dead, and from the ground there blos-soms red, life that shall——

CCLI# 7098754

To God Be The Glory

Key = D

Original Lyrics: Fanny Jane Crosby
Additional Lyrics & Music: Jonathan Veira/Mark Edwards
Arr: Jonathan Veira & Mark Edwards

SONG NOTES

by Jonathan Veira

I SURRENDER ALL

Written in 1896 by a man with a really great name - Judson Wheeler Van De Venter! This song is a passionate gospel song coming out of the American tradition rather than traditional English hymnody.

A lilting pace should be taken in this simple hymn, building always to the chorus where harmonies, vocal as well as instrumental, can be a real asset. In this arrangement, lead *if you can* from the keyboard to give solidity. Can be used to great effect as a solo piece with the congregation joining on the chorus.

I WILL SING THE WONDROUS STORY

F H Rowley, a Baptist minister, wrote these words in 1886 and they became very popular with evangelist Ira D. Sankey. They have stood the test of time, still being included in hymn collections and sung in churches today.

The old tune remains but I have made the tempo more of a fast Irish jig rather than the temperate respectful tempo usually taken. I would love this to be taken as one in the bar rather than the slightly plodding three in a bar – hence the little theme in the first four bars to kick it off as a hymn of energetic praise. Play the theme as many times as you like with whatever instrument can play it!

JOYFUL JOYFUL, WE ADORE YOU

Beethoven began this hymn's journey with his 9th Symphony (choral) and the melody known as *Ode to Joy*. It has been my personal joy to sing this as a soloist with a large orchestra and now with the words of Van Dyke and Hodges, we sing of the joy of the God of Love. In 1911, this poem came to the notice of the church and has been described as one of the most joyous expressions of hymn lyrics in the English language

In our version of *The Hymns Project* you will notice that it is just a little bit funky! A band will really make this song go with a swing. If you want the whole version as appears on the recording then that is also available for you to have and to practice!

JUST AS I AM

In 1875 Charlotte Elliot wrote this memorable hymn used so much by the late Billy Graham after he was converted in a service in Charlotte, USA!

A well-known preacher asked Charlotte if she was a Christian. Sick and in a lot of pain, she took offence at his question and retorted somewhat rudely! However, a few days later she returned to him and asked *how* to become a Christian...he said to her 'Come just as you are'. A number of years later, the words came back to her and she wrote the now famous poem 'Just as I am'.

The new tune is written in the modern song/ballad style with a new chorus. It is suitable for a band or just keyboard and/or guitar accompaniment.

LOVE DIVINE, ALL LOVES EXCELLING

Possibly the most popular of Charles Wesley's hymns first appeared in 1747 in a book somewhat dauntingly called "Hymns for those that seek, and those that have redemption". Not the snappiest of titles but a truly outstanding example of a hymn encompassing the Trinitarian nature of God – Father, Son and Holy Spirit.

The new tune is to be sung at a 'moderato' tempo with a real sense of dynamic variance – loud and soft – probably slowing slightly in the final verse. Sing heartily and with passion on this most beautiful of themes.

O FOR A THOUSAND TONGUES TO SING

In 1739, a year after his conversion, Charles Wesley wrote this to celebrate the momentous event. He originally wrote a set of 18 stanzas of which we come in at verse 7 – O for a Thousand! The previous words are now forgotten but the hymn we now sing is one of the most popular of the Wesleyan output. It is believed that the source was his friend Peter Bohler who said to Charles "Had I a thousand tongues I would praise Him with them all!"

The new tune is written to enable guitarists to be able to play it easily and for an accompanying band to find the groove. A four-bar motif at the beginning launches the song and is to be played between the new chorus and each verse. This gives the congregation something to hook onto and prepare for the next verse.

O LOVE THAT WILL NOT LET ME GO

A deeply moving song written in 1882 when minister George Mathieson was 40 years old. He wrote it on the eve of his sisters' wedding recalling his own devastating rejection from a fiancée some 20 years previous who felt unable to commit to a man diagnosed with blindness. In just 5 minutes, George wrote the words without stopping. The theme reflects the love of God in all its colourful and imaginative glory - here is the love that will never let me go.

The musical style in this new tune is of a ballad with an added chorus and suitable for solo or group singing. It is to be sung with passion, commitment and assurance at a steady pace. Guitar and piano would make an ideal accompaniment with drums joining in the first chorus.

TO GOD BE THE GLORY

One of our most prolific female hymn writers Fanny Crosby, who was blinded as a one-year-old after an unfortunate incident, wrote over 9000 hymns and songs including this very popular song c 1872. 'To God Be The Glory' celebrates the simple tale of the Gospel - it is a song of theology and celebration.

With this new tune, a small band is useful but not essential. Sung with joy and verve at a steady pace, this new music to timeless words will prove an added dimension to an already very popular hymn.

FOR INFORMATION AND BOOKING DETAILS VISIT

www.jonathanveira.com